D1370387

INVEST KIDS™

GOODS AND SERVICES

Gillian Houghton

PowerKiDS press™

New York

Published in 2009 by The Rosen Publishing Group, Inc.
29 East 21st Street, New York, NY 10010

First Edition

Editor: Joanne Randolph
Book Design: Julio Gil
Photo Researcher: Jessica Gerweck

Photo Credits: Cover, back cover, pp. 9, 13 Shutterstock.com; p. 5 © David De Lossy/Getty Images; p. 6 © Tim Platt/Getty Images; p. 10 © Somos/Veer/Getty Images; p. 14 © Stockbyte/Getty Images; p. 17 © www.iStockphoto.com; p. 18 © Ariel Skelly/Getty Images; p. 21 © flashfilm/Getty Images.

Library of Congress Cataloging-in-Publication Data

Houghton, Gillian.
   Goods and services / Gillian Houghton. — 1st ed.
      p. cm. — (Invest kids)
   Includes index.
   ISBN 978-1-4358-2775-2 (library binding) — ISBN 978-1-4358-3210-7 (pbk.)
ISBN 978-1-4358-3216-9 (6-pack)
   1. Commerce—Juvenile literature. 2. Consumer goods—Juvenile literature. 3. Service industries—Juvenile literature. 4. Purchasing—Juvenile literature. 5. Selling—Juvenile literature. I. Title.
   HF5392.H68 2009
   381—dc22
                                        2008039976

Manufactured in the United States of America

Contents

Buy Me!   4

I Need It! I Want It!   7

Needs Come First   8

Plan for Your Wants   11

Get a Job!   12

The Goods   15

At Your Service   16

The Producers   19

The Consumers   20

Shop Smart!   22

Glossary   23

Index   24

Web Sites   24

Buy Me!

We live in a country in which most **businesses** are owned and run by people who want to make a **profit**. These businesses compete, or fight, for **customers** using **billboards**, posters, and ads on television. Most businesses say they offer the best services or make the best **products**. They say that they sell these services or products at the lowest prices.

As customers, we get to decide what products and services we want to buy. With so many products for sale, it can be hard to pick. It is important to learn how to be smart shoppers and how to spend our money carefully!

This family is comparing different toys in the toy store. There are so many choices for toys and other products, it can be hard to decide which product is the best!

5

We all need clothing, but clothes can be a want, too. Sometimes we buy more clothes than we really need or pick clothes that are more costly because we want a certain look.

I Need It! I Want It!

We spend our money on two kinds of **purchases**. There are the things that we need in order to live and there are the things we want to own or enjoy. Things we need include food, clothing, and **shelter**, while things we want are things we can live without, such as toys.

For every need, however, there are many different products for sale. When you go shopping for a winter coat, you may find a plain coat that meets your needs and a more expensive coat that you want much more. You need a winter coat, but you want the winter coat that costs more. You may even make yourself believe that you need the more expensive coat.

Needs Come First

Our basic needs are the things we need to live. The list of basic needs changes over time and from one group of people to another. Most people agree that to live in the world today, you need food, shelter, clothing, running water, and electricity.

Most of us cannot **afford** to buy the things we need and all the things we want. This is why it is important to buy the things we need first. If you buy the things you want first, you may run out of money before you can buy the things you need. That new bike will not do you much good if you cannot afford to buy food or pay for a place to live!

We need healthy food, such as fruits and vegetables, to live. At the supermarket, we need to make sure we buy healthy food first, before we buy less healthy snack foods.

Have your family help you learn about the different bills and coins with real money or play money. Then you will know how to add up and keep track of your money.

Plan for Your Wants

After you have paid for the things you need, you can begin to think about the things you want. You may not have enough money to buy the things that you want right away. You can make a budget, or a plan for how to earn, save, and spend your money. Save your money over time, setting aside a little every week or every month.

After saving enough money for the things that you want, you might decide you do not want those things after all! Your wants will change over time, so your budget will change, too.

Get a Job!

To earn money, we work. There are many jobs different people do. Some people work as firefighters, mail carriers, or doctors, and others work cutting hair or cleaning houses. Different jobs require different amounts of education and training, and the people who do these jobs are paid different amounts for their work.

You may be too young to get a regular job, but there are still ways for you to earn money. Ask the people in your family or in your neighborhood if there are chores, or little jobs, that you can do for money. Some kids mow lawns and others walk dogs. You might like to sell cold drinks or homemade cookies on the sidewalk.

Raking leaves during the fall months can be a good way to make money. When it snows, you can shovel driveways, and you can cut grass in the spring and summer.

Next time your mother shops online, ask her if you can look at the Web site with her. She will likely use a credit card, like the one shown above, to pay for her purchases.

The Goods

There are two kinds of products. There are goods and there are services. Goods are things that you can touch. A glass of lemonade and a cookie are goods you might sell in your neighborhood. The clothes you wear, the books you read, and the food you eat are all goods. Another word for "goods" is "merchandise."

Merchandise is generally sold in a store, where it is displayed, or shown, for customers. Stores on the Internet are becoming more common, too. Customers look at pictures of products online. If they decide to buy something, the goods are sent directly from the **warehouse** to the customer.

At Your Service

A service is work done by one person for another person. When you mow your neighbor's lawn or walk his dog, you are providing a service. When you get your hair cut at the barbershop, your teeth cleaned at the dentist's office, or your food brought to your table at a diner, you must pay for these services. Another word for "service" is "labor."

We pay a certain amount of money for these services, and if we think the work was well done, we may decide to pay a little extra. This extra money is called a gratuity or tip.

These children have started a neighborhood recycling service sorting their neighbors' recyclable goods. Each neighbor agreed to pay them some money for this service.

This woman grows fruits and vegetables and sells them at a farm stand. A farmer with a larger farm might sell her produce to a supermarket or to restaurants.

The Producers

The people who make and sell goods and services are called producers. In turn, producers may count on other producers for materials, or parts of the finished product.

For example, think about the hamburger for sale at the restaurant, or place you go to eat, in your neighborhood. The restaurant cooks and sells the hamburger, but it must buy the **ingredients** from many different producers. The restaurant buys the raw, or uncooked, meat from one producer. It buys the pickles from another producer and the cheese from yet another producer. It takes many different producers to bring the hamburger to your plate.

The Consumers

The people who buy goods and services are called consumers. Consumers have many choices, and together they agree on the value of a product. If a product costs too much money, or its value does not match its cost, consumers will not buy it. There is no **demand** for that product at that price. The producer must lower the price or stop selling the product.

On the other hand, many consumers believe that a product is only valuable if it costs a lot of money. Other consumers place more value on products that are **rare**. Producers must keep all these things in mind when they decide how much to make of a product and how much to charge.

Every time you go shopping with your family, you are being a consumer. A smart consumer compares products and makes sure he is buying things at a good price.

Shop Smart!

There are so many goods and services to pick from, but it is a good idea to think about what you buy. Is it something you need or something you want? You must always take care of your needs before your wants. Can you afford it? Is it worth the price? Can you find the same product at a different store for a lower price? Will you still want it in a week or in a year? Can you wait for the product to go on sale, or do you need it right away?

What you decide to buy and what you decide not to buy can say a lot about what you value. Are you a smart consumer?

GLOSSARY

afford (uh-FAWRD) To be able to pay for.

billboards (BIL-bawrdz) Large signs with ads for products printed on them.

businesses (BIZ-ness-ez) Groups of people who work together to make and sell things.

customers (KUS-tuh-murz) People who buy goods or services.

demand (dih-MAND) The want or need for a good or service.

ingredients (in-GREE-dee-unts) Parts of a mix.

products (PRAH-dukts) Things that are produced.

profit (PRAH-fit) The money a company makes after all its bills are paid.

purchases (PUR-chus-ez) Things that have been bought.

rare (RER) Not common.

shelter (SHEL-ter) A place that guards someone from weather or danger.

warehouse (WER-hows) A building in which goods are stored until they are needed.

INDEX

A
ads, 4

B
bike, 8
billboards, 4
businesses, 4

C
clothing, 7–8
consumer(s), 20, 22
customer(s), 4, 15

D
demand, 20

E
electricity, 8

F
food, 7–8, 15–16

M
money, 4, 7–8, 11–12, 16, 20

N
need(s), 7–8, 22

P
price(s), 4, 20, 22

product(s), 4, 7, 15, 19–20, 22
profit, 4
purchases, 7

S
shelter, 7–8
shoppers, 4

T
television, 4
toys, 7

W
warehouse, 15

WEB SITES

Due to the changing nature of Internet links, PowerKids Press has developed an online list of Web sites related to the subject of this book. This site is updated regularly. Please use this link to access the list:
www.powerkidslinks.com/ikids/services/